PETS FROM AROUND THE WORLD

COLORING + ACTIVITY BOOK

Thanks to your purchase, we are able to
donate books to kids in long-term hospital care,
foster care, and homeless shelters.

www.caravanshoppe.com

TOOLS YOU'LL NEED:

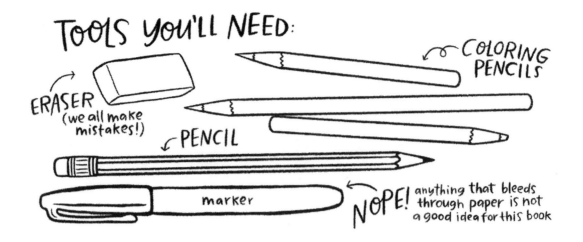

ERASER (we all make mistakes!)

COLORING PENCILS

PENCIL

marker

NOPE! anything that bleeds through paper is not a good idea for this book

MIKE   ALMA   HOLLY

ABOUT THE AUTHORS

We are MIKE & ALMA LOVELAND and HOLLY SPARKS. We are ARTISTS and we are PARENTS, and basically we wanted to create activity books that would make our kids think we're cool. (So far it's working!) We hope that you have as much fun with this book as we had making it for you!

First Printing: 2020

ISBN: 978-1-7361663-1-4

Caravan Shoppe books are available at special discounts when purchased for promotions, fundraising, and educational use. Special editions or book excerpts can also be created. For details, contact hello@caravanshoppe.com.

Illustrated, written, and designed by Mike Loveland, Alma Loveland, and Holly Sparks.

Printed in the United States of America.

www.caravanshoppe.com

WHOA! THERE'S A LOTTA PETS IN HERE! Can you find all 38?
☐ 3 TARANTULAS ☐ 5 CATS ☐ 2 DOGS ☐ 1 LLAMA ☐ 4 BIRDS

☐ 7 REPTILES   ☐ 6 FISH   ☐ 10 SMALL MAMMALS
(1 tortoise, 3 snakes, 3 lizards)   (1 sugar glider, 1 rabbit, 1 hamster, 1 gerbil,
3 guinea pigs, 1 mouse, 1 rat, 1 hedgehog)

TYPES OF PET OWNERS

aaaaaaa-CHOOO!!

ALLERGIC

OKAY!!! I'll feed you! Just after I finish one more level...

NEGLECTFUL

I picked up the poop!

RESPONSIBLE

I will DEFINITELY feed her EVERY DAY, clean up after her, train her well, take care of her health, spend time playing together every day. She will be totally my responsibility and I will never forget to do anything...

OVER-PROMISER

I will do ANYTHING for my pet human!

♥ **BFF** ♥

Umm... Someone else can hold it now!

NON-PET PERSON

SMOTHERER

I love you! I love you! I love you! I love you! I LOVE YOU!

If I get a leopard gecko, it will need live food... so I guess I would have to breed my own roaches!

COOL!

ASPIRING

DOGS vs CATS: THE ULTIMATE DEBATE

Dogs are the VERY BEST PET.
Only a fool would think that
CATS are the ultimate snugglers!
DOGS are the warmest & cuddliest.
It is undeniably FALSE that
YOU CAN TRUST a cat to be there for you.
Here's the TRUTH about cats:
They're sneaky.
And dogs?
100% LOYAL.
Pet experts agree that cats are
nothing but trouble.
Everyone knows that dogs are
intelligent, funny & emotionally supportive.
Cats are
QUITE THE OPPOSITE.
DOGS are the #1 companion.
You can't possibly believe that
CATS are the VERY BEST PET!

ARE YOU CONVINCED?
WAIT!! Now read it from bottom to top!

HOW DO RABBITS TRAVEL?

FINISH THE WORDS BELOW TO FIND THE ANSWER!

iconic rabbit food
CA _ ROT
5

rabbit poop. AKA
_ ELL _ TS
7   11

a home for rabbits
_ UTCH
3

can train rabbit to use a
LITTER _ OX
1

clip your rabbit's
_ AILS
10

rabbits have long
E _ RS
4

popular rabbit food
L _ TTUCE
6

adorable cotton
T _ IL
9

rabbits like company!
SOCIA _
8

an herb for rabbits
PARSLE _
2

‒ ‒ ‒ ‒ ‒ ‒ ‒ ‒ ‒ ‒ ‒
1 2 3 4 5 6 7 8 9 10 11

RHINOCEROS BEETLE

costs about 500 to 8000 yen
That's 5 to 80 dollars!

Some VERY FANCY beetles
can cost nearly $1000.

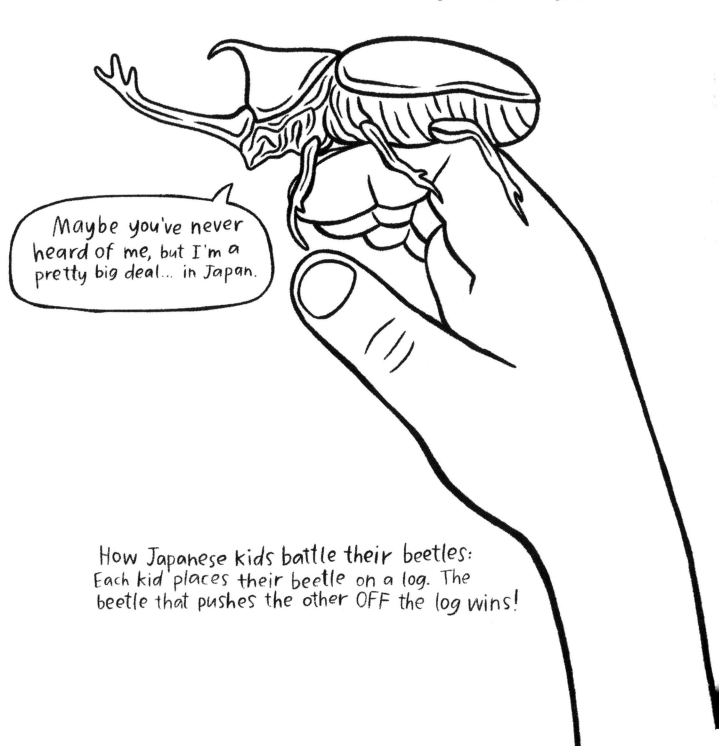

Maybe you've never heard of me, but I'm a pretty big deal... in Japan.

How Japanese kids battle their beetles:
Each kid places their beetle on a log. The
beetle that pushes the other OFF the log wins!

can you spot TEN differences?

The AFRICAN PIXIE FROG is NOT SMALL!

The nickname "pixie" comes from their latin name: Pyxicephalus adspersus

needs to be fed crickets, earthworms, hornworms, silkworms, or small rodents!

ME HUNGRY!

EXOTIC ANIMALS

A PET KEPT IN HUMAN HOUSEHOLDS THAT YOU PROBABLY THINK BELONGS IN THE WILD IS CONSIDERED AN EXOTIC PET! *Remember! Just because you CAN own some of these pets doesn't mean you SHOULD!

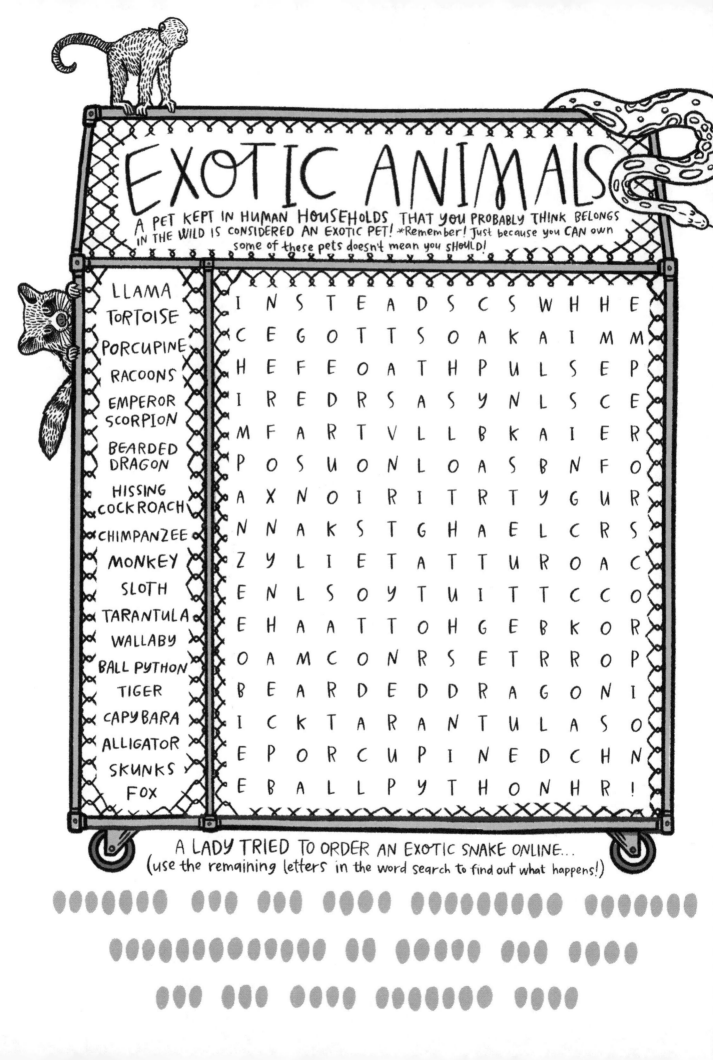

Word list:
- LLAMA
- TORTOISE
- PORCUPINE
- RACOONS
- EMPEROR SCORPION
- BEARDED DRAGON
- HISSING COCKROACH
- CHIMPANZEE
- MONKEY
- SLOTH
- TARANTULA
- WALLABY
- BALL PYTHON
- TIGER
- CAPYBARA
- ALLIGATOR
- SKUNKS
- FOX

Word search grid:

```
I N S T E A D S C S W H H E
C E G O T T S O A K A I M M
H E F E O A T H P U L S E P
I R E D R S A S Y N L S C E
M F A R T V L L B K A I E R
P O S U O N L O A S B N F O
A X N O I R I T R T Y G U R
N N A K S T G H A E L C R S
Z Y L I E T A T T U R O A C
E N L S O Y T U I T T C C O
E H A A T T O H G E B K O R
O A M C O N R S E T R R O P
B E A R D E D D R A G O N I
I C K T A R A N T U L A S O
E P O R C U P I N E D C H N
E B A L L P Y T H O N H R !
```

A LADY TRIED TO ORDER AN EXOTIC SNAKE ONLINE...
(use the remaining letters in the word search to find out what happens!)

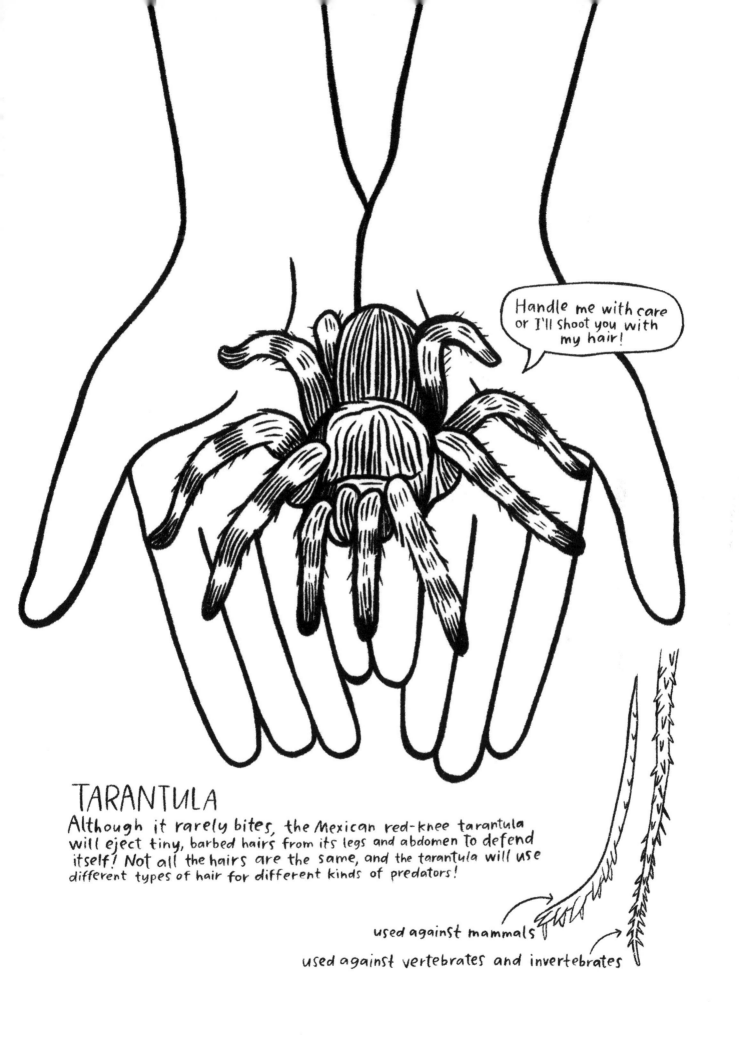

TARANTULA
Although it rarely bites, the Mexican red-knee tarantula will eject tiny, barbed hairs from its legs and abdomen to defend itself! Not all the hairs are the same, and the tarantula will use different types of hair for different kinds of predators!

used against mammals

used against vertebrates and invertebrates

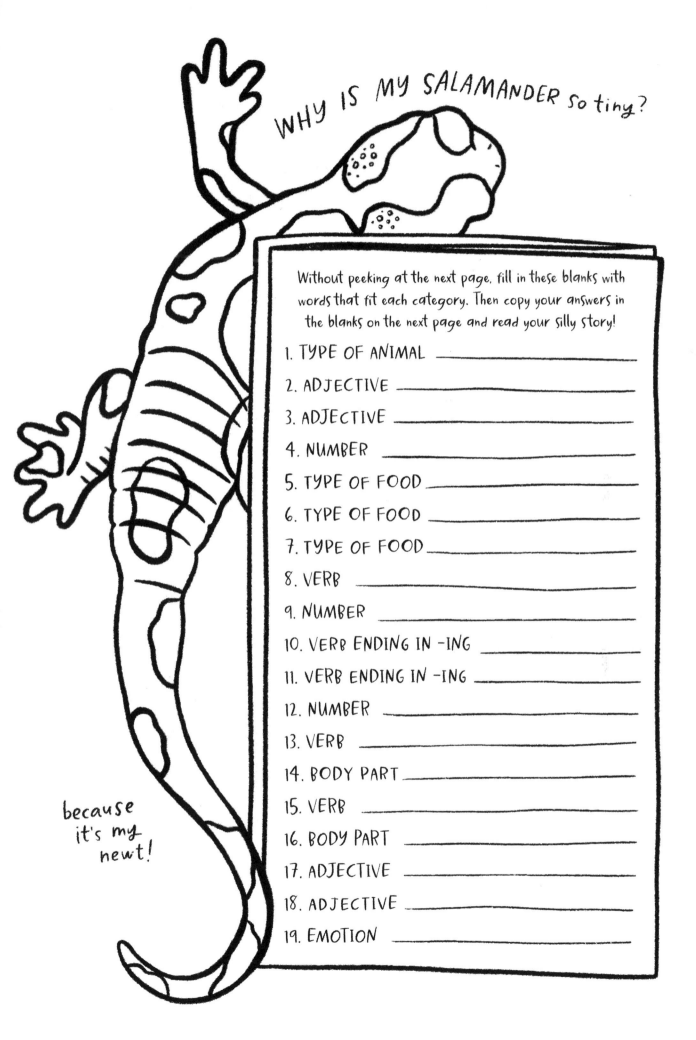

WHY IS MY SALAMANDER so tiny?

Without peeking at the next page, fill in these blanks with words that fit each category. Then copy your answers in the blanks on the next page and read your silly story!

1. TYPE OF ANIMAL _____

2. ADJECTIVE _____

3. ADJECTIVE _____

4. NUMBER _____

5. TYPE OF FOOD _____

6. TYPE OF FOOD _____

7. TYPE OF FOOD _____

8. VERB _____

9. NUMBER _____

10. VERB ENDING IN -ING _____

11. VERB ENDING IN -ING _____

12. NUMBER _____

13. VERB _____

14. BODY PART _____

15. VERB _____

16. BODY PART _____

17. ADJECTIVE _____

18. ADJECTIVE _____

19. EMOTION _____

because it's my newt!

PET CARE INFO: _____
1. type of animal

(Fill this out using your answers on the previous page.)

Congratulations on your new _____, and welcome to the
1. type of animal

_____ world of caring for your _____ pet! First, let's talk
2. adjective   3. adjective

about FOOD! Your pet needs to eat _____ times a day. You should
4. number

only feed your pet _____ or _____. Do not be
5. type of food   6. type of food

tempted to feed your pet _____ because it will cause your pet
7. type of food

to _____ uncontrollably. Next up, SLEEP! Make sure your pet gets
8. verb

_____ hours of sleep EVERY DAY. Insufficient sleep will lead to
9. number

behavior issues like _____ and _____.
10. verb ending in -ing   11. verb ending in -ing

Do you have more than one _____ living in your home?
1. type of animal again

BE CAREFUL! This pet is known to reproduce quickly, and within a month

you may have _____ pets in your home! Now let's talk about
12. number

GROOMING. Every day, you must _____ your pet's _____
13. verb   14. body part

and _____ your pet's _____. AND FINALLY, let's talk about the
15. verb   16. body part

BOND you have with your pet. Every day, find time to gaze into your

pet's _____ _____ eyes, and you'll find the _____
17. adjective   18. adjective   19. emotion

between you will grow strong.

BETTA FISH don't make great roommates because they will try to EAT EACH OTHER. But, they actually do well swimming with other, smaller fish.

bettas are jumpers and can jump out of their tank!

I need a new roommate. I DEFINITELY don't know what happened to the last one...

males create bubble groups on the surface of the water to attract females even if there is not one in the tank!

PIG

This pet is SMART!

Pigs are considered the 4TH most intelligent animal (after humans, primates, and dolphins).

They are easy to train, but their intelligence can be challenging. It's like having a 2-3 year old as a pet.

The pets on these pages appear at their ACTUAL SIZE

Place your hand next to the animals on these pages to imagine what it might be like to hold them.

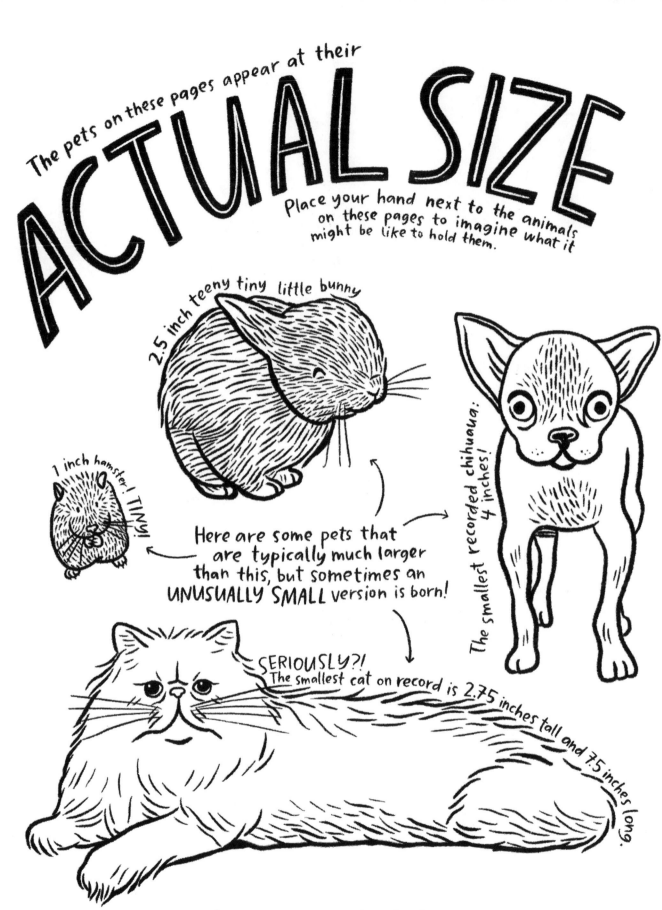

2.5 inch teeny tiny little bunny

1 inch hamster! TINY!

The smallest recorded chihuahua: 4 inches!

Here are some pets that are typically much larger than this, but sometimes an UNUSUALLY SMALL version is born!

SERIOUSLY?!
The smallest cat on record is 2.75 inches tall and 7.5 inches long.

BONUS! With this book open, turn it sideways.
The length of this open book (17 inches) is the height of the SMALLEST HORSE!

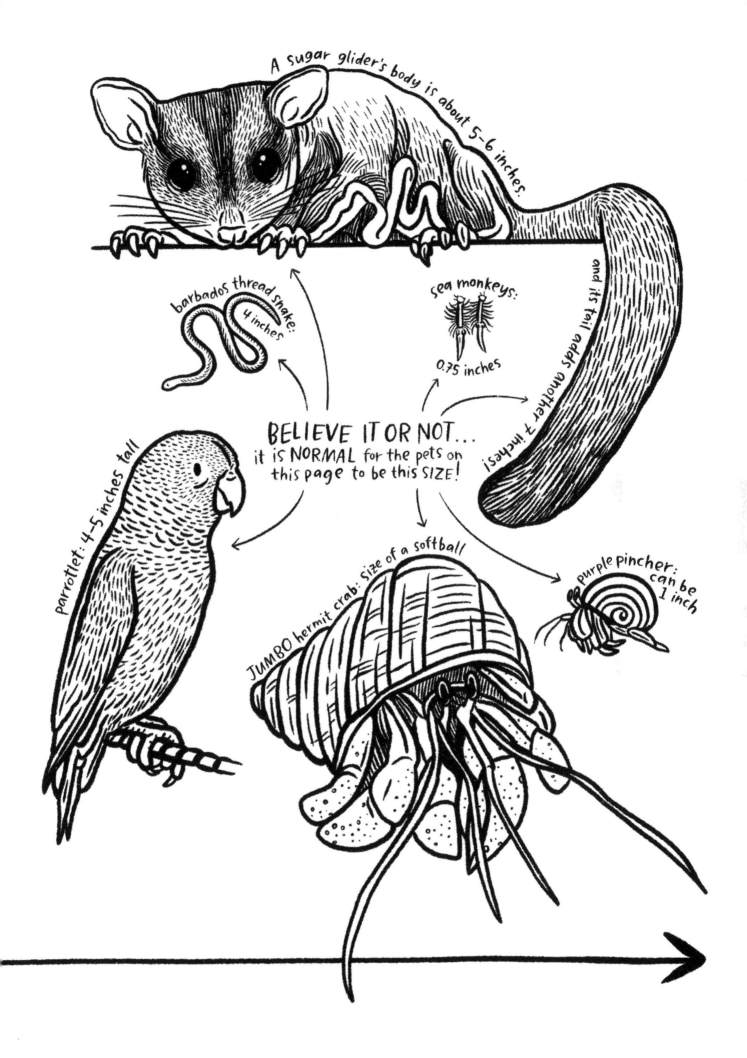

A sugar glider's body is about 5-6 inches.

and its tail adds another 7 inches!

barbados thread snake: 4 inches

sea monkeys: 0.75 inches

BELIEVE IT OR NOT...
it is NORMAL for the pets on this page to be this SIZE!

parrotlet: 4-5 inches tall

JUMBO hermit crab: size of a softball

purple pincher: can be 1 inch

WHEN A HEDGEHOG SMELLS SOMETHING NEW, IT...

1. licks and bites the new thing.
2. Starts foaming at the mouth.
3. spreads the foamy saliva all over its body.

WHY? No one really knows for sure...

What's the story? Fill in the bubbles to show what's happening here!

DOGS can smell 100,000 times better than humans and hear 10 times better than humans!

BUT! Humans see more color than dogs (dogs see mostly gray, blue and yellow).

Dogs and humans have been companions for over 15,000 years.

Do you smell that?

PET BIRDS

```
P W H A T D L O V E B I R D O
E P D O V E C O C K A T O O Y
A P O O U P A R A K E E T G E
C T I I W P C O C K A T I E L
O A H O C E A N Y O U F T C C
C R N L N E O R S S A I O P A
K P A A O U P R R R O N U M I
E T I R R R S H W O I C C A Q
C A T G O Y I P A H T H A C U
L M A S E S H K A L A L N A E
E A R ? O E A E R U P E W C
C Z E T T H N L A E R S T T R
T O C O N U R E L T T O A L O
U N K S Y O U R H A E A T D W
S A F R I C A N G R A Y O F F
```

LOVEBIRD	MACAW		PEACOCK
CONURE	POICEPHALUS	DOVE	CAIQUE
PARAKEET	COCKATOO	CANARY	AFRICAN GRAY
TOUCAN	ROSELLA	ECLECTUS	PARROTLET
CROW	AMAZON	PIGEON	COCKATIEL
LORIKEET		FINCH	PIONUS PARROT

USE THE LEFTOVER LETTERS TO FILL IN THESE BLANKS

●●●● ●● ●●● ●●● ●●●● ●●● ●●●●● ● ●●●●● ●●●● ● ●●●●●
● ●●● ●●●● ●●● ●●●● ●●●● ●●● ●●●

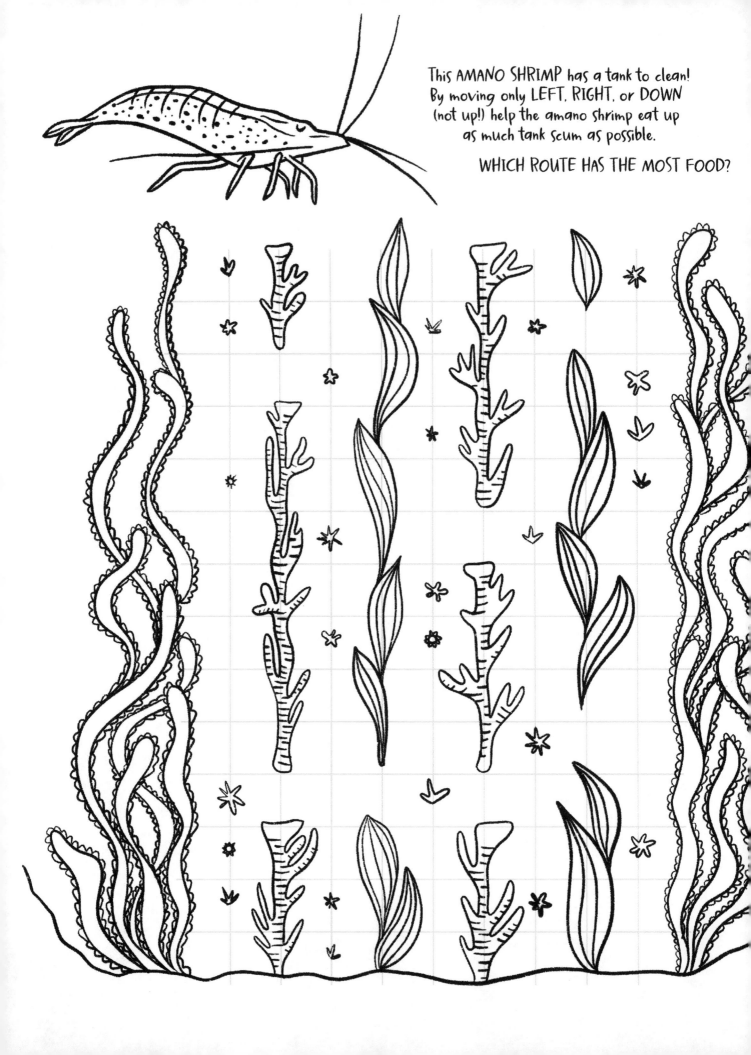

This AMANO SHRIMP has a tank to clean!
By moving only LEFT, RIGHT, or DOWN
(not up!) help the amano shrimp eat up
as much tank scum as possible.

WHICH ROUTE HAS THE MOST FOOD?

WHICH CATS FAILED THEIR TEST?

FINISH THE WORDS BELOW TO FIND THE ANSWER!

baby cat
KIT _ EN
11

used for scratching
CL _ WS
1

a cat that has no home
STR _ y
12

a cat says
M _ O W
6

unhappy sound
_ ISS
13

cough it up
_ AIR BALL
8

description word for cats
FE _ INE
3

a batch of baby cats
_ ITT _ R
2   9

hairless cat
SP _ YNX
5

highly sensitive hairs
WHI _ K _ RS
14   10

it killed the cat
_ URIOSI _ y
7   4

_ _ _   _ _ _   _ _ _ _   _ _ _ _ _
1 2 3   4 5 6   7 8 9 10   11 12 13 14

GREEN TREE PYTHON

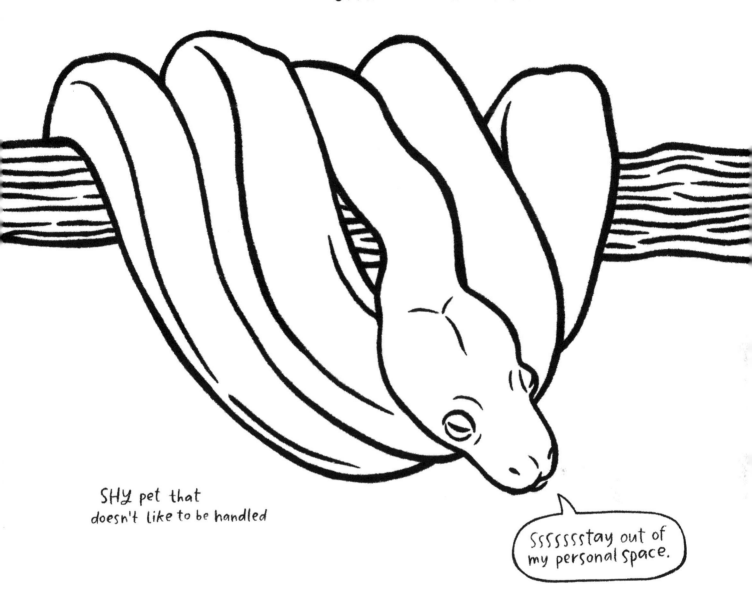

SHY pet that
doesn't like to be handled

Sssssssstay out of
my personal space.

CHANGES COLORS! They are born maroon, red, or
yellow, but turn BRIGHT GREEN as they mature.

Expensive! $300 - $1500+

POPULAR RODENT PETS

most—BUT NOT ALL—of these pets
are RODENTS.

Look for clues in the illustrations to help you
find the FOUR PETS that are not actually rodents.

SUGAR GLIDER

RAT

GUINEA PIG

COMMON DEGU

AFRICAN DORMOUSE

FERRET

RABBIT

Where in the world did these pets come from?

SOLVE EACH EQUATION AND FIND THE ANSWER ON THE MAP

chinchilla
19 + 6

guinea pig
9 − 7

sugar glider
29 − 24

red-eared slider
1 x 1

gray parrot
121 ÷ 11

bearded dragon
3 x 3

tree frog
7 x 6

Scarlet macaw
99 ÷ 33

emperor Scorpion
18 ÷ 3

hamster
16 + 16

cockatiel
9 x 4

gerbil
18 − 14

veiled chameleon
49 ÷ 7

SOME TORTOISES LIVE MORE THAN 200 YEARS...

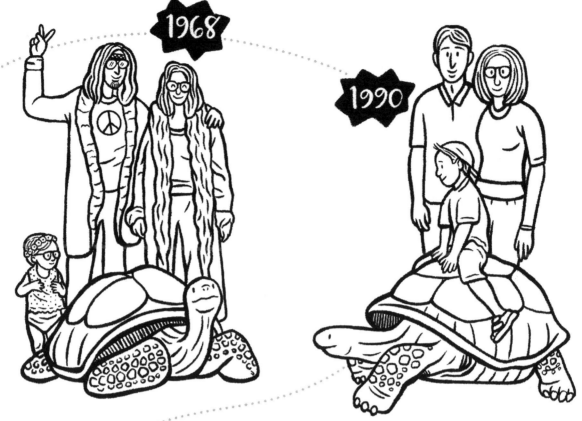

CAN *YOU* TAKE CARE OF A PET TORTOISE THAT LONG?

HOW TO DRAW A CAT USING LETTERS!

two big upside down Vs
one small v

∧ ∧
ˇ

one BIG S

two round, deep Ws

follow closely around
your S shape!

draw a line to connect
the letters

Add details!

Go
teach it to
your friends!
right MEOW!

ペット・カフェ

動物

Japan has PET CAFES, where you can grab a drink and relax
with a variety of pets, including owls, birds, cats, dogs, pigs... and even capybaras!

90 GALLONS, WIDTH=24, HEIGHT=36, DEPTH=24

3 GALLONS
WIDTH=9
HEIGHT=11
DEPTH=7

30 GALLONS
WIDTH=18, HEIGHT=24, DEPTH=18

HOME SWEET HOME

Taking care of pets means providing the right home. Read the requirements below each pet to determine which enclosure is the best fit. Draw each pet inside its ideal home.

5 inches

ONE TARANTULA

minimum tank width must be three times the leg span of the spider

must have hideouts

ONE BETTA FISH

tank must be at least 3 gallons

FIVE HERMIT CRABS

tank must be at least 10 gallons, plus 2 gallons for each crab

must contain at least 6 inches of sand

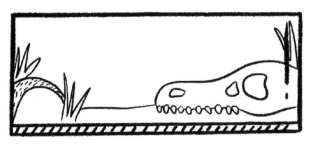

7 GALLONS
WIDTH=20
HEIGHT=8
DEPTH=10

20 GALLONS
WIDTH=30
HEIGHT=13
DEPTH=13

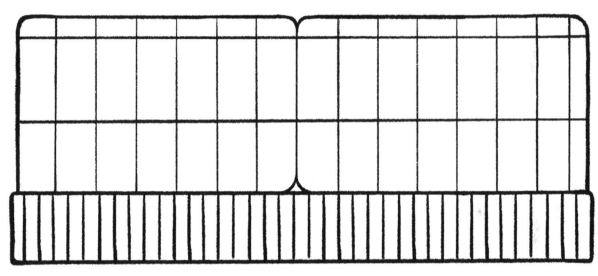

WIDTH=40, HEIGHT=16, DEPTH=30

ONE GUINEA PIG

enclosure must be at least
1080 square inches (W x D)

enclosure should have wire cage
to allow free airflow

THREE CRESTED GECKOS

height of tank must be
greater than width

tank must be at least 29 gallons

ONE VEILED CHAMELEON

height of tank must be
greater than width

tank must have a screen
to allow good airflow

How to draw ADORABLE EYES...

1

2

3

4

...now add adorable eyes to these pets!

HERMIT CRABS can LOSE LEGS or CLAWS when they are sick!

BUT... take good care of your crab and it will GROW BACK its missing limbs!

Hermit crabs pee through their faces.

CHIENGORA is yarn made from dog fur

let's say you own 4 CHOW CHOWS and 1 POMERANIAN.

one day of brushing your dogs results in 1 ounce of fur

a paper grocery bag holds 8 OUNCES of fur

1 OUNCE of dog fur can be spun into 50 yards of yarn

needs 800 yards of yarn

400 yards

how many days will it take to collect enough fur to make a small sweater?

how many bags of fur are needed to make a scarf?

needs 2000 yards of yarn

are 4 bags of fur enough to make this poncho?

After years of careful breeding, you have created the

ULTIMATE PET!

Discover your pet breed by following the CODE below:

BIRTH DATE

1. Bearded
2. Crested
3. German
4. Golden
5. Bengal
6. Exotic
7. Himalayan
8. Giant
9. Miniature
10. Common
11. Spotted
12. Green-cheeked
13. Snowy
14. Speckled
15. Long-tailed
16. Short-hair
17. Long-hair
18. Pygmy
19. Hairless
20. Naked
21. King
22. Albino
23. Teddy
24. Mountain
25. Toy
26. Curly-coated
27. Wire-haired
28. Fancy
29. Great
30. Chinese
31. American

BIRTH MONTH

JAN: Cocker
FEB: Labra
MAR: Bull
APR: Yorkie
MAY: Dwarf
JUNE: Day
JULY: Land
AUG: Hermit
SEPT: Gray
OCT: Hedge
NOV: Night
DEC: Hissing

FIRST LETTER OF FIRST NAME

A: Hound
B: Doodle
C: Gecko
D: Poo
E: Matian
F: Shepherd
G: Dragon
H: Pig
I: Pug
J: Retriever
K: Tail
L: Sphynx
M: Hare
N: Hog
O: Skink
P: Pincher
Q: Conure
R: Macaw
S: Snake
T: Rex
U: Dog
V: Bird
W: Cat
X: Crab
Y: Fish
Z: Tortoise

_____   _____   _____

BIRTH DATE   BIRTH MONTH   FIRST LETTER
                                        OF FIRST NAME

draw your ULTIMATE PET here!

DID YOU KNOW you can rent LLAMAS for
your WEDDING? These llamas come perfectly
dressed for the occasion and are ready for hugs, cuddles,
and PHOTOS with the happy couple and their friends.

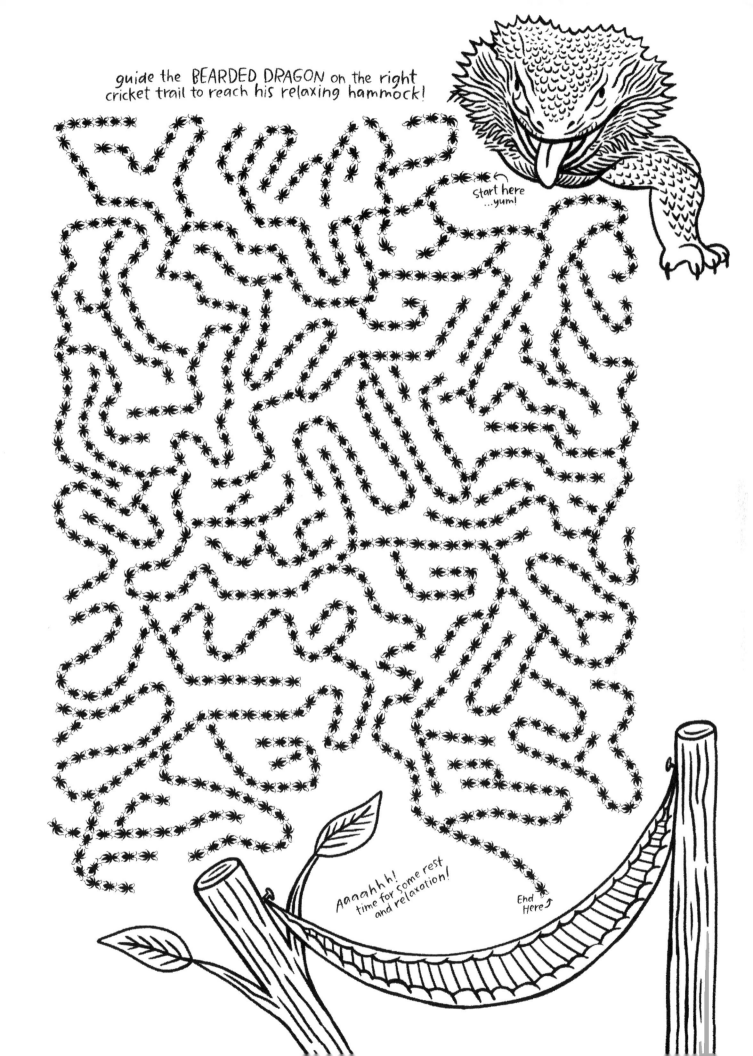

guide the BEARDED DRAGON on the right cricket trail to reach his relaxing hammock!

Start here ...yum!

Aaaahhh! time for some rest and relaxation!

End Here

If you own a CAPYBARA you will need...

1. More than one. Capybaras are very social!

2. Lots of outdoor space. They are huge, weighing 77-150 lbs.

→ ⧼BIGGEST⧽ rodent in the world

3. A pool for swimming.

4. A fence. They are speedy and like to run away!

webbed feet for swimming

Capybaras can hold their breath under water for FIVE MINUTES

How to draw a COCKATIEL

STEP ONE

With a pencil, lightly draw this jelly bean...

STEP TWO

Add lines for beak, eye, head feathers, tail, wing, and legs...

STEP THREE

Fill in the details.

STEP FOUR

MORE DETAILS! MORE! MORE!

G'day mate!

TURTLES are NOT silent.

A pet turtle is not as loud as a dog or cat, but it can make noises like chicken-clucks, or tiny dog-barks, depending on the species.

EXCUSE ME? I may be quiet, but I can still hear you.

Turtles don't have ears, but they're not deaf. Thin flaps of skin cover internal ear bones, which receive vibrations and low-frequency sounds.

kibble made from meat, grains, fruits & vegetables

flakes

unseasoned table scraps

WHAT GOES IN MUST COME OUT

Feeding and cleaning up after your pet are both important! Follow each path to see some typical foods and some typical poop-cleaning routines!

DOG

HERMIT CRAB

LEOPARD GECKO

sift out poop/pee daily; refresh litter monthly

vacuum bottom of tank weekly; refresh water monthly

pick up poop in yard daily; pick up poop during walks immediately

paté made from meat, minerals & vitamins

live insects

seeds, nuts, fruits, vegetables

GOLDFISH

PARROT

CAT

remove poop daily; deep clean tank weekly or monthly

scoop poop 2x weekly.

deep clean tank monthly

DAILY NEWS

replace liner of cage daily; deep clean cage weekly.

WHERE'S THE CHEESE?! It's true: mice will eat cheese (let's be honest... they will eat about anything!), but a good pet owner will feed their mouse a variety of foods! Help this little mouse get the foods he needs!

If you can't imagine life without your cat or dog but you know your pet is getting old...

(and you have an extra $50,000 in your bank account)

SCIENTISTS can CLONE YOUR PET!

Does that mean you are getting the EXACT SAME PET? Well, not really. Let's explain it this way:

These kids are IDENTICAL TWINS.

They are NOT the SAME PERSON but they DO have the same DNA

These dogs are CLONES. Like identical twins, they have the same DNA, but they are NOT the SAME DOG. They will be similar but also have some differences!

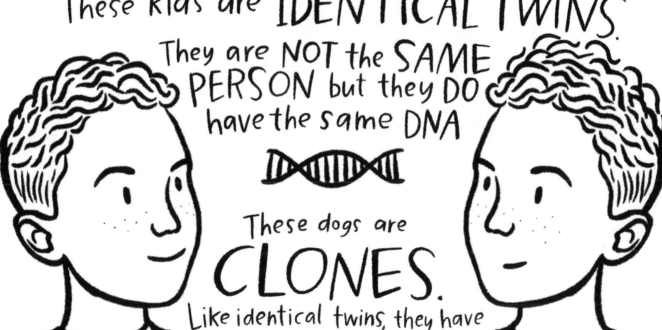

find
FIVE
tiny
differences
between
each
pair of
clones

FERRETS are like STINKY CATS...

- uses a litterbox
- gets hairballs from licking itself
- playful and curious

BUT SMELL FOUL & MUSKY!

(many owners will have their ferrets surgically "de-scented")

Illegal pet in California & Hawaii!

ACROSS
2. Uses tiny hairs to defend itself
7. Be sure to "de-scent" this MUSKY pet!
8. Can GROW BACK missing limbs
9. Popular insect pet in Japan
10. Has skin flaps over its ears

DOWN
1. Born with a full set of teeth
3. Needs a night light to sleep
4. Attracts females by blowing bubbles
5. Foams at the mouth when exploring new things
6. Weighs as much as a stick of butter

psst! Every animal in this crossword is represented in this book! Don't know the answer? Flip back a couple pages!

Ever notice how some pets and owners look a lot alike? Match up all the owners with their lookalike pets!

TURN THE PAGE TO FIND THE ANSWERS TO THIS BOOK!

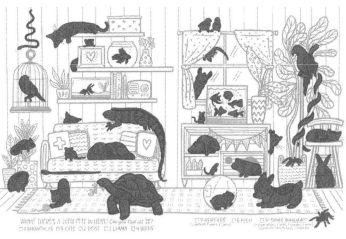

WOAH! THERE'S A LOTTA PETS IN HERE! Can you find all 38?
☐ 9 REPTILES ☐ 5 FISH ☐ 10 SMALL MAMMALS
☐ 3 TARANTULAS ☐ 5 CATS ☐ 2 DOGS ☐ 1 LLAMA ☐ 4 BIRDS

MIRACLE MIKE
SIDE SHOW ⟶ THIS WAY

ILLEGAL

Not all pets are legal! Unscramble the letters below to discover some pets that might be illegal, depending on where you live.

A TRAIL LOG **ALLIGATOR**

TAB **BAT**

PAROLED **LEOPARD**

HOD EGG HE **HEDGEHOG**

NINE PUG **PENGUIN**

MY KENO **MONKEY**

FINISH THE WORDS BELOW TO FIND THE ANSWER!

CAR ROT   PELLETS

HUTCH   LITTER BOX   NAILS

EARS   LETTUCE   TAIL

SOCIAL   PARSLEY

BY HAREPLANE

can you spot TEN differences?

EXOTIC ANIMALS

instead she got some feathered scarves
unfortunately it turns out that
the boa cons tricked her!

PET ADOPTION

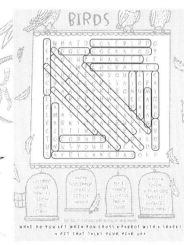

BIRDS

WHAT DO YOU GET WHEN YOU CROSS A PARROT WITH A SHARK?
A PET THAT TALKS YOUR HEAD OFF

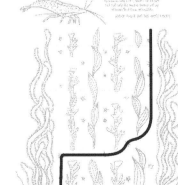

WHICH CATS FAILED THEIR TEST?

FINISH THE WORDS BELOW TO FIND THE ANSWER!

KITTEN   CLAWS   STRAY

MEOW   HISS   HAIR BALL

FELINE   LITTER   SPHYNX

WHISKERS   CURIOSITY

ALL THE CHEETAHS

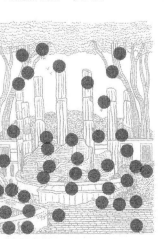

CLUES: all rodent illustrations have grass instead of rocks
all rodent illustrations are smiling
all rodent illustrations have dot eyes

16 DAYS   1 BAG   NO

find FIVE tiny differences between each pair of clones

	H							
T	A	R	A	N	T	U	L	A
	M							
	S		H		C		S	
B	T	F	E	R	R	E	T	
E	E		D		C		G	
T	R		G		K		A	
T		H	E	R	M	I	T	C	R	A	B
A			H		I		G	
F			O		L		L	
R	H	I	N	O	C	E	R	O	S	B	E	E	T	L	E
S			G				D	
			T	U	R	T	L	E
							R	

ACROSS

DOWN

THE ENDS

Do your siblings and friends want
to do these activities, too?

Wish you could do your favorite activity again?

GET 50% OFF A PRINTABLE VERSION OF THIS BOOK!

ENTER DISCOUNT CODE AT CHECKOUT:
6VUXE8CV

scan this with
a smart phone
camera

OR visit: caravanshoppe.com/products/books-pets

Check out our other books!

We're already working on our next books, and we love your feedback and requests! Send us an email at hello@caravanshoppe.com.

WANT MORE?

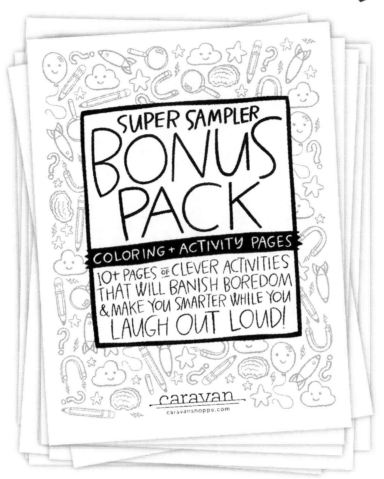

Sign up to receive occasional email updates, and we'll send you this ≡SUPER SAMPLER BONUS PACK≡ of all-new activities!

scan this with a smart phone camera

OR visit:
http://bit.ly/33JHJhF

Made in United States
Troutdale, OR
01/30/2024

17301369R00046